The Chri

Or, Scientific and Religious Journal

(Volume 1)

January, 1880

Various

Editor: Aaron Walker

Alpha Editions

This edition published in 2021

ISBN : 9789355344885

Design and Setting By
Alpha Editions
www.alphaedis.com
Email – info@alphaedis.com

THE CONFLICT

The pyramids, temples and palaces of Thebes are monuments of the ancient intellects of our race. Great thinkers only were capable of giving to the world the Vedas, the Apollo Belvidere and the Parthenon. The arts and astronomy of Egypt harmonize very poorly with the idea that modern scientists have all the wisdom and intelligence known in the history of the ages. Among the wonderful characters of olden times we find Epictetus, Josephus, Strabo, Pliny, Seneca, Virgil, Aristotle, Plato, Tacitus, Thucydides and Herodotus.

The "Speculation of Evolution of Species" was advocated among the Greeks six hundred years before the birth of Christ. Two thousand and three hundred years ago the entire system of German philosophy, along with modern pantheism, was advocated by the Buddhists and Brahmins.

In many very important respects the ancients were in advance of us, especially in the arts, and we can not boast of superiority in either letters or philosophy. "The gentlemen of modern materialistic schools do not compare favorably with Plato and Cicero in the elevation and reverence of their opinions." "Science has certainly made some advancement, but where is the warrant for the boasting" of sciolists of modern times?

Buddhists taught the most perfect outline of materialism in general. "They believed in a supreme force, but denied the existence of a Supreme Being. They rejected inquiry into first causes as unscientific," maintaining that facts alone were to be dealt with in all our investigations.

The Brahmin contemplated the moment when his spirit would flow back into the great "Pantheistic Being."

Modern materialists say, "We deal only with facts." "We never speculate." The Buddhists, and the unbelievers who figure so boastingly upon the rostrum in modern times, speak alike. They say: "As many facts and second causes as you please, but ask no questions about first causes; *that* is unscientific." We should ask no questions (?) about the invisible. They have been very true (?) to their own principles.

There is nothing speculative (?) in the hypothesis that General George Washington was evolved from a crustacean. There never was a more absurd and wild speculation. It is an old speculation. Anaximander, who lived six centuries before Christ, advocated the assumption. His words are the following: "The sun's heat, acting on the original miry earth, produced filmy bladders or bubbles, and these, becoming surrounded with a prickly rind, at length burst open, and as from an egg, animals came forth. At first they were ill-formed and imperfect, but subsequently they elaborated and developed." This has the genuine ring of the language of modern unbelievers.

Christianity, in its beginning, had to encounter this "speculation" along with the current literature and philosophy of a civilization which was semi-barbarous and centuries old, but it triumphed over all, and in the third century it triumphed everywhere. Since that time one effort has been made upon the part of paganism to regain her former strength in the old world. Julian made that effort. He tried to revive and establish the supremacy of pagan thought by the power of the state. Subsequent to this it disappeared in the east, and has only plead for toleration in the west. But the dark ages came on in all their hideousness, and unbelief developed itself about the close of the fifteenth century, all over Europe. Paganism, as the result, was fostered near the bosom of the church. The fifth Lateran Council proclaimed anew the tenet of the imperishability of the spirit of man. The Padua University adopted a system of materialism taught in the works of Alexander, of Aphrodisias. A form of pantheism known in the philosophy of Averroes soon became a center of skepticism.

In the latter part of the seventeenth century modern unbelievers began their assaults. Lord Herbert and Hobbs in England, Spinoza in Holland, and Bayle in France.

In seventeen hundred and thirteen Anthony Collins published a discourse for the encouragement of a "clique" called "Free-thinkers." This discourse was thoroughly answered by Bently. In seventeen hundred and twenty-seven Woolston made an effort to rationalize the miracles out of existence, interpreting them after the style of Mr. Strauss. Three years later Tyndal got out his dialogue called "Christianity as old as the Creation." The world received in return for this "Butler's Analogy of Natural and Revealed Religion." In seventeen hundred and thirty-seven Morgan's "Moral Philosophy" made its appearance, claiming the sufficiency of the moral law without any other religion. Warburton's "Divine Legation of Moses" was gotten up in reply to this philosophy. Thomas Chubb wrote a discourse upon reason, and got out a few other small tracts denying the utility of prayer, and calling in question the truth of the Scriptures of both Testaments, in the line of Morgan's philosophy. Bolingbroke, ignorant of the law, "that the greatest good of the greatest number is to be sought after," even at the expense of the lives of a few wicked Canaanites, assailed the justice and the benevolence of the Bible God after Col Ingersoll's style, and boldly avowed that the miracles of the New Testament never transpired; said, "If they did occur they attested the Revelation." Voltaire lived between 1694 and 1788. He made himself busy in France, while Bolingbroke and Tyndal and Woolston, and Hume and Morgan were at work in England. Then Didoret, of France, made his appearance upon the stage as a bold defender of Atheism. Next comes D'Holbach, the leading author of the "Systeme de la Nature," which came out in 1774. Its object was to strike down the idea of a God, of an intelligence separate from matter, of free-will, and of immortality. Didoret and others are accused of assisting in getting this book before the world. Rousseau lived in those times, and assailed Christianity after the manner of Hume. To all these enemies of Christianity we must add Condillac, who originated the materialistic philosophy of France.

Gibbon and Paine came into notice after Bolingbroke, and the terrible strife continued. Christianity was pronounced dead, and a prostitute was chosen to impersonate the "Goddess of Reason" in the national convention. God being dethroned in France, we should naturally look there for the "absolute liberty" which unbelievers talk so much about. But how was it? Were the people without a religious nature? Could they think more freely? Were they in any sense better off? No, they "followed the prostitute into the church of 'Notre Dame' in a grand procession and seated her upon the high altar, where she was worshiped by the audience." This was the result of the labors of all the authors to which I have called your attention. It was a wonderful gain? In all the public cemeteries this inscription was read: "Death is an eternal sleep." Cabanis, Destutt de Tracy and Volney close up the seventeenth century, but just about this time the "Critique of Pure Reason," a work which is the bed-rock of modern metaphysics, makes its appearance. According to its teachings there are no realities in the world.

The struggle is passed in England. In France all are dull, drowsy. In Germany all are hungry for the food that satisfies unbelievers. The "Critique of Pure Reason" was followed by the labors of Fitche. He was succeeded by Schelling, and he by Hegel. All forms of torture must be added to this account of the conflict if we would get a glimpse of the strength of the Christian religion and of the religious element in man's nature, from the amount of resistance which they have defied. Eusebius says, "The swords became dull and shattered" under Diocletian. "The executioners became weary and had to relieve each other." This would not look as though Christianity would take the throne in four score years, but it did in spite of all those cruel murders. Through Constantine it became the state religion of the Roman Empire. Paganism crumbled down and Christianity triumphed over all the opposition of the old world. The books of the Old and New Testaments have all been thoroughly tested, over and over in the fiery furnace of criticism, but Christianity still lives to bless the hearts of widows and orphans; to bless the disappointed and disconsolate. To-day there are more Christians in the world than ever before.

What has unbelief to give to the people of our age more than it offered centuries ago? Nothing! Nothing!! Nothing!!!

"There is nothing new under the sun."

THE BIBLE—THE BACKGROUND AND THE PICTURE.

This book is admired and respected above all others for its antiquity, its usefulness, its conflicts, and character. It has been expressly denominated "The book of books." Its professions are such that no reasonable man can consistently lay it aside without giving it a careful examination. The nature of every question determines its claims upon our intelligence. If it professes to involve only a small interest its claims are not so pressing.

The questions of the Bible hold in their principles the present and eternal interests of our humanity, and therefore challenge the attention of the world. Thousands of the wisest and best men of the ages have been intensely interested in its contents. Its great influence and reputation are evidences of its trustworthiness, and of the consistency and intelligence of those who give it their attention; for sensible men do not disregard questions of great importance. This book contains a record of many ugly, dark and wicked deeds, known in the lives of wicked men and nations, with imperfections and apostacies of individuals in high places. This is what we must look for in a book of its pretensions. It professes to contain a revelation of God and his will to man. The ugly, wicked, licentious, and bloody things constitute the background of the picture, representing man in all his ways. It is also shaded with all there was, and is, of moral and noble character in the human. God with his attributes, as the true, grand and glorious Bible picture, shines out through this human background. The justice of God, with his love, long suffering and tender mercies, his approbation and disapprobation, must in the very nature of things be revealed in connection with human character as it presents itself in iniquity and crime, in piety and virtue, both individual and national, in order that the revelation may be complete, full and perfect. The history of men and nations must also be true, sufficiently full to call out, in the divine dealings, all there is in the divine character; otherwise, the revelation would be partial and imperfect.

No physician ever revealed his skill without his patients. No court has ever revealed its justice without its cases. The doctor's dealings with his patients measure the extent of his known skill. Allowing that he understands himself and the conditions of his patients perfectly, and does his whole duty, the revelation of his skill must be perfect, to the full extent of its connection with the diseases treated. So it is with the revealed justice of the court. This rule is a necessary law, governing all revelations of character, both human and divine; otherwise we are left in the dark with reference to the true character of the one who makes the revelation. Our common sense is such that we are always led astray by improper action, unless our superior wisdom enables us to know that the action is improper. Improper action upon the part of a doctor reveals imperfect skill; on the part of the court it reveals imperfect justice, if it is not an entire want of skill and justice.

No such imperfection belongs to our God; therefore the revelation which he made needs only to be understood and it will never mislead us. These great principles of common sense are to be applied in the revelations of God to the nations as the God of nations. Such being the case, we have a very interesting field of thought before us in the bloody scenes that are known in the history of nations, as it is given in the Bible. Where is the morality and righteousness of the wars of which we read? Where is the justice and goodness of God in the bloody wars of Israel? Where is the righteousness of capital punishment? A great many persons say, in their ignorance, there is no righteousness in those things. Friend, travel slowly over this ground. "Take the shoes off thy feet, for it is holy ground." Go into the Bible and look! God is there. You knew it not. Principles never change. Circumstances change and necessitate changes of law, but that which was right at any time in the history of our race is right at all times, under the same circumstances. Is there such a thing as morality carried into public relations? Is there such a thing as jurisprudence? Yes; jurisprudence is morality carried into public relations in the following law: "That course of conduct which pertains to the greatest good of the greatest number is right." This law is of universal application. It belongs to men in all their relations, both public and private, collectively and individually. In the relation of the State to its citizens it taxes them for the support of government, it fines, imprisons and puts them to death for crime. In the relation of nation to nation it imposes tariffs and declares war, filling history with scenes of blood and woe. The common sense of mankind approves this law, and the Bible declares it just. Wars were approved of God, when they were for the greatest good of the greater number. It was upon the same principle that all the divine judgments were administered, from the destruction of the Antediluvians down to the overthrow of Jerusalem by Titus.

This law is the substratum in moral righteousness, underlying all that is right. Such is its wonderful latitude and longitude that, in order to carry it out, it sometimes becomes necessary to tilt a nation into a sea of blood and replace it with a better people. Unbelievers and skeptics who admit this are guilty of wresting Bible facts from their proper places and testing them upon the plane of morality, regardless of the laws of jurisprudence.

This erroneous method of reasoning leads the minds of many ignorant and unsuspecting persons away from the right ways of God. The guilty reasoner justifies taxation, fines, imprisonment and wars in the history of his own country.

It sometimes seems cruel to carry out this great moral principle of which we are treating; it is nevertheless right, and men who abuse its facts and turn things upside down are guilty of opposing the right.

Unbelievers are guilty of selecting from the Bible all that can be tortured out of its place in the laws of jurisprudence and made to look ugly out of its proper relations, and are continually holding such things up before the people, turning them into ridicule, and at the same time they have been through all the bloody scenes of war and justify themselves, wishing to be known in many instances as Major, General or Colonel. We have some such in our own country. They seem to have never learned that many things which are good for humanity are very ugly out of their proper relations. I am glad that God has revealed himself in the jurisprudence of nations, for the facts given inspire confidence in rulers and officials, strength to judges upon the bench, and nerve to warriors who are acting with direct reference to the "greatest good of the greatest number."

A history of God in his dealings with states and nations in order to a perfect revelation of himself necessitates a history of states and nations so far as it is necessary to make known the approbation and disapprobation of God in connection with all that may ever enter into national or state character. Without this we would find states and nations where God did not see fit to show himself. We must find him wherever we find man, approving or disapproving. This is just what we do in the Bible. We do it in no other book. But let us ever remember that all that is wicked had its origin with wicked men and demons, and that the Divine Being, with all his attributes, appears in the foreground in all his relations to men and their conduct, as the grand Bible picture shining out through all the darkness and gloom, surrounded with the virtues and noble deeds of all his worshipers, and that he is building up and throwing down as his righteous judgment approves or disapproves. This revelation of God is like the sun at noonday bursting through dark and heavy clouds and blessing the earth with its rays. In making this revelation, which is related negatively or affirmatively to all there is in human history, God saw fit to communicate his will through man, and in his own language, except in the gift of the great charter of the national existence of the children of Israel and the great foundation truth of the church of God. These he uttered with his own wonderful voice.

Was it reasonable to expect a revelation from God? Is it necessary to the greatest good of the greatest number? If so, it is a thought at once involving the moral character of God and necessitating a revelation of himself. In answering these questions intelligently we must look after the demands for such a communication. Where shall we find them? Answer, in the wants of our humanity. Here two kinds of light are needed for two pair of eyes in order that we may be happy in two respects. First, physical light for the physical eyes, in order to the enjoyment of physical life in a material world. Second, the light of knowledge for the eyes of the understanding, in order to the enjoyment of spiritual life in a spiritual world. It is universally conceded that there are means provided in nature to meet man's physical wants and adaptations that manifest the wisdom that belongs to God; also, that it would have been the work of a demon to create man with these wants, like so many empty vessels, without any provision to satisfy or fill them. Without those supplies our suffering would be great and our wretchedness unendurable. Is there no liability to mental suffering? Are there no spiritual wants consequent upon the nature of mind?

Is it not unreasonable to allow that "Infinite wisdom" provided for all our physical wants and left our spirits with all their demands, like so many children away out in the darkness without hope, uneasy, restless, always dissatisfied, and ever trying to get into the possession of the knowledge of the unseen and future, without one ray of mental light shining out from the heavens upon our relations to perfect our condition and declare the glorious goodness of an all-wise Creator? Volney says, "Provident nature having endowed the heart of man with inexhaustible hope, he set about finding happiness in this world, and failing in his efforts, he set out in his imagination and created a world for himself, where, free from tyrants, he could have all his wrongs redressed and enjoy unsullied bliss." This is Volney's account of the origin of religion, the tap-root of the tree. It contains a most wonderful concession, one that Tyndal made when he said, "There is a place in man's psychological nature for religion." Is there a place in man's physical nature for bread and meat, for food of every variety that man's soul desires? Do we attribute all the mercies of physical life to a supreme intelligence? Has that intelligence created us and left us endowed with "Inexhaustible hope," to be disappointed forever, and the only result, the "imaginary" creation of the Christian's happy heaven. But Volney makes another grand concession in the quotation which I have given, and that is the nature of the Christian's future world in its relations to wrongs as well as tyrants, neither are to exist there. That the Christian's religion, with its beautiful world, does fill up the soul's demands is a fact unintentionally conceded by Volney, and known throughout the land in the contentment and bliss and heroism of the dying Christian. In this hope alone man's spiritual wants are met. This, with all that pertains to it, is in the revelation that God has made to our race. How could this be made? I answer, it was made by the spirit of God. "Holy men of old spake as they were moved upon by the Holy Spirit." This is what we call *inspiration.* This word is a translation of "*Theopneustos,*" which is from "Theos," *God,* "pneuma," *spirit, Spirit of God.* Is it reasonable to allow that this revelation could be given by the spirit of God through holy men? I will let an infidel answer this question. Bolingbroke said, "It is just as easy to comprehend the operation of the spirit of God upon the mind of a prophet in order to give his will to us as it is to comprehend the operations of our own spirits upon our physical nature in order to an expression of our own thoughts." Has such a revelation been made? From all we know of man, his wants, and the adaptation of means in nature to those wants, we are driven to the conclusion that it has, presenting the means adapted to our spiritual wants so perfectly as to enable us to realize fully what Volney declares our very nature, as creatures of hope, impelled us to create "in our imaginations for ourselves." There is no consistent ground that any man can occupy between Christianity and Atheism. And if there is no God, "nature," or the "forces," or whatever lies behind them, to which they belong, as the manifest energies of the same, call it what you may, has made a very unreasonable, bungling mistake in giving in the very nature of man's mind an empty vessel that is to be filled only by the false whims of the imagination of an ever restless and dissatisfied spirit, which, in that case, is to be eternally disappointed and plunged deeper down by the realization of the fact that all its anxieties and hopes were only so many misleading demons.

In order to a perfect revelation of God to man it was necessary that the entire page, the "background" as well as the "foreground," or the human as well as the divine, should be truth, and in every case, all the truth that was necessary to enable man to realize and understand the whys and wherefores of the divine procedure; and also to call out in word or action the Divine Being in all his relations to the conduct of the children of men. Such a record is found in the Bible, given to us by men who were impelled and borne by the Holy Spirit when they wrote and spoke. But it was not necessary that anything upon the dark human "background" of this picture should have its origin with God; it was only necessary that, having originated with man, men or demons, it should be put to record just as it was in all its heinousness and wickedness in order that we might see the true character of God in his relations to it. If a wise physician should undertake to make himself known to the world he would not give us a history of all he did with every patient, and at the same time fail to give us just so much of the true history of each patient as would be necessary to enable us to understand him in all that he did, for both stand or fall together. So it is in the Bible revelation of God to man. Take away the "background" of the picture, and the picture itself is destroyed. That which skeptics in their ignorance are always trying to ridicule is just as essential to a revelation of God in his justice, purity, love and power as the word of God himself. That is to say, the revelation has an objective as well as a subjective side. The subjective is God in his attributes, and the objective is man in his works. It was the objective that drew out the subjective, because all was done for the objective. Take either side away and the revelation ceases to exist. On the subjective side all is of God in its origin, is charged up to him, being spoken by him, and in his name, or done by him, or by his authority. The indices to this great truth are in these or similar phrases, "Hear, O, Israel, thus saith the Lord, thy God," "Thus saith the Lord," "And the Lord said," "The Lord spake, saying," "The Lord said unto me," "The word of the Lord came unto me," "The Lord commanded," "The burthen of the word of the Lord to," "The Lord answered, saying." We are not authorized to charge, as many through their ignorance or wickedness have done, all that we read about in the Bible to God as the author. The words and doings of wicked men and demons are truthfully recorded there, and they are often licentious and blasphemous. The words and doings of good men and angels are there, and the words and doings of God are there. We are authorized to charge to God's account that only which is spoken in his name, or by his instructions, along with that which was done by him, or by his authority, or approved by him. When we get outside of these common-sense thoughts in our interpretations of Bible history we are acting upon our own responsibility, and are liable to be found doing violence to the divine will. If we contradict the record we call in question the veracity of the spirit which controlled the writer, whether the statement relates to God, man or demons. But this statement does not apply to mistranslations, for it is one thing to contradict an uninspired translator, and another altogether to contradict the statement of one controlled by the spirit of God. We fearlessly assert that the Bible is just the book that common-sense and reason demands that it should be in order to contain a revelation of God to man. We would as soon attempt to destroy the divine and lovely side, as change its character, so far as to take from its pages its record of wickedness, misery and woe, for it amounts to the same thing. One more question of importance bearing on this subject demands our attention, and that is the question of miracles. Men have, without any authority from the Bible, treated all miracles as violations of natural law. But it would be well for us to determine the extent of our knowledge of natural laws before we thus dogmatize. That which we call miracle may be in perfect harmony with law that lies just beyond our knowledge. Omniscience seems to be a necessary qualification for such theorizing as asserts that miracles are violations of the laws of nature. Omnipotence is an essential attribute of the Ruler of the universe. But in order to its existence, the Infinite one must be above the laws which he has established, able to take hold of those laws and handle them as he sees proper, otherwise he is not all-powerful. On the simple plane of nature we get lost. Who can account for "Partheno Genesis," or generation without any known sexual organs, which obtains in the animal kingdom. "The spirit of God moved upon," "brooded over" the face of the great deep and life filled the waters. "The Holy Spirit overshadowed the Virgin" and the Nazarene was begotten. The original expresses the same idea in both cases. Scientists who are radical materialists admit this wonderful feat in the animal kingdom as a natural affair, and yet, without any authority from the Bible, speak of the birth of Christ as the result of "Miraculous conception," in the sense of a violation of natural law. What natural law is violated in "Partheno Genesis?" With me it is allowable that a thousand more just such beings might be, and if necessary to the accomplishment of the great purposes of God, would be produced under the same circumstances and by the same instrumentalities. The feature of the question of miracles which bears on the subject of a divine revelation must now be considered. It is this, would a book containing such a record as that which we have in the Bible, except the record of miracles, reveal God in his attributes to our world? We lay it down as a correct proposition that we must have creative and life-giving power manifested in order to a revelation of God.

If the Bible contained no record of the exercise of powers above the human it would reveal only a human God, which would be no God; and common sense would declare, "It is a book treating of, and presenting man in his attributes." Those facts upon its pages which are in the power of God alone confirm, that is, make sure, the revelation of God to man. Without this feature of the book common sense would have at least one good excuse for rejecting its claims. The Master recognizes this fact in the saying, "If I do not the works of my Father believe me not, but if I do, though ye believe not me, believe the works, that ye may know and believe that the Father is in me and I in him." Here we have the fact of "God revealed in the flesh," evinced by the works which the Savior performed. The foundation of faith, or the obligation to believe, is identified with those works. They were a greater evidence of his divinity than the words of any prophet, although those words were the words of the Divine Spirit. Jesus said, "I have greater witness than that of John, for the works which the Father hath given me to finish, the same works that I do, bear witness of me that the Father hath sent me." "If I had not done among them the works which none other man did, they had not had sin; their rejection of my claims would be justifiable but for the fact that my divinity is demonstrated in the works which I do." The same thought accompanies the introduction of the gospel of Jesus Christ in the preaching of the Apostles. Paul said, "Our gospel came not unto you in word only, but in power, and in the Holy Spirit." "They went everywhere preaching the word; the Lord working with them and confirming the word with signs following." The confirmation was not in the simple fact that miracles were wrought, but in their character. The miracles of Christ were not in the power of false prophets, magicians, or demons. They were in the power of God. Peter said, "God anointed Jesus of Nazareth with the Holy Spirit and with power," and that "He went about doing good, and healing all who were oppressed of the devil; for God was with him." The presence of God was manifested in his miracles.

The question is often asked, "Why were they not continued throughout the Christian dispensation?" Answer: If they had been continued, they would have lost all their power over the mind by becoming ordinary, and then they would cease to have any bearing whatever in the establishment of a divine proposition. It was not necessary to continue them beyond the witnesses whose testimony closed up the revelation of God. "A covenant once confirmed no man disannulleth or addeth thereto." A continual repetition of the evidence of confirmation was not necessary in order to give faith in a communication already confirmed and left in a historic age for the faith of the world. It is true of sense that the continual sensuous experience causes the object experienced to lose its controlling power, but the opposite is true of faith. So he who knew best what man's nature required ordained that the just should walk by faith and not by sense. And to this end he confirmed "once" the revelation of himself and his will, and left it in the world as his witness to produce faith. "If we receive the witness of men the witness of God is greater; for this is the witness of God which he hath testified of his Son. He that believeth hath the witness in himself; he that believeth not God hath made him a liar, because he believeth not the *record* that God gave of his Son." Is it not a dangerous thing to make God a liar? Is it not a great insult? All unbelievers are thus guilty before God. Our Savior did not speak unadvisedly when he said: "He that believeth not shall be condemned."

"Life and immortality are brought to light through the Gospel." Is it not strange that dying men will reject the motive of life? "This is the record, that God hath given to us eternal life, and this life is in his Son; he that hath the Son hath life, and he that hath not the Son of God hath not life." Jesus "came to his own and his own received him not, but as many as received him to them gave he power to become the sons of God." Will we possess him through faith and live, or shall we make God a liar, die in our sins, be condemned and banished from the presence of God and the glory of his power?

The practice of dating from the Christian era was first introduced about the year 527, by Dionisius, surnamed "Exiguus," but better known as Deny's le Petit, a monk of Scythia and a Roman abbot. It was not introduced into Italy until the sixth century. It was first used in France in the seventh century; it was universally established in France in the eighth century. It was used in England in 680; it was in general use in the eighth century. The years of the Christian era are described in ancient documents as the years "of Grace," of "the Incarnation," of "our Lord," of "the Nativity," etc.—*Chambers.*

The cardinal virtues are Justice, Prudence, Temperance and Fortitude. *Cardinal* signifies, in a general sense, principal or pre-eminent. It comes from the Latin word *cardo*, a hinge. Take cardinal things away from any science and its foundation is gone. Everything in science turns upon cardinal things, as the word *cardo* signifies.

A FUNERAL ORATION

BY COL. G. DE VEVEU.

Of the future, the hereafter, we are as ignorant as we are of the infinite conditions through which we have passed during the eternity which has preceded our brief present existences. If we could know the history of our past we might get a glimpse of our future; but no message ever reached man from beyond the grave. The past is a mere sealed book, the future is a blank. No records are left to us save those written in the rocks and the evidences brought before our senses; they tell their own stories. Whence came we? Whither are we tending? Ah! who can tell? Some profess to know, but they know not. Where have last summer's roses gone? What will become of yon dry leaf, torn from its parent stem by this wintry blast? Like us they disappear and are merged into the ocean of matter from which they are evolved, ready to be re-combined into new forms of beauty; for although individual existences perish, matter is imperishable; having had no birth it will have no death. Like time and space, it is infinite and eternal. Brought forth into this world without being consulted, we are hurried out of it without our consent. Like that leaf, which was the hope of spring, the pride and glory of summer, we are rudely torn away, the sport of destiny, to return to the elements of nature from which we spring—dust to dust. The past is beyond recall; the future is veiled in obscurity and in doubt; the present alone is ours.

The above is from the Boston *Investigator*. It has gone the rounds of the press, and it is regarded as a very fine literary production. But all is not gold that glitters. This oration was delivered as a tribute of respect to the memory of Mrs. Boulay. It is a curiosity when viewed from the speaker's standpoint. The man was evidently broken down in the presence of death. I have sometimes thought it would be well for the unbelievers to adopt the custom of delivering funeral sermons, for it is certain, from all that is known of man, that no strong defense of unbelief, nor even a respectable presentation of it, is made in the presence of death. When an unbeliever speaks at his brother's grave of the "rustling of wings," I intuitively think of the old trite saying, "It is but one step from the sublime to the ridiculous." That step is from the "rustling of wings" to "infidelity." Col. G. Veveu, in the above oration, sticks close to his unbelief, but smashes *his science*. If our incredulous friends will continue to respect the dead enough to remember them with an oration at their graves, I think it will be but a short time till the people all over the country will see the hollow, empty, good-for-nothing character of unbelief.

Mr. Veveu says, "Although individual existences perish, matter is imperishable; having had *no birth (italics mine)* it will have *no death*." A wonderful discovery! *Matter had no birth*; organisms are born. They existed, however, prior to their birth. The matter that composed them existed before it entered into organic forms. The living element, spirit, or whatever you please to name it, took hold of the elements of matter and built the organism. The life existed before the organism. Why should it perish with it? Matter exists before birth and after death. Spirit also exists before birth and after death. Why affirm the eternity of matter and deny the eternity of spirit? These unbelievers, being materialists, advocate the one substance theory. Yet they talk about the "unknown" which they know, and know it to be the "invisible," the "wonderful," the life, and the cause, at least, of all intelligence and order. They are compelled to deify this. Does this pass out of being with death? Does matter pass out of being with death? No, nothing passes out of being except the organic form. The body returns to the dust, *as it was*, and the spirit to God who gave it. Next, we have this statement with reference to matter, "Like time and space, it is infinite and eternal." Why? The answer is, because it can not be annihilated; death has simply destroyed an organization, changed the condition of matter, the matter of the organism, and changed the relations of the intelligent, living spirit; neither matter nor spirit ceases to be. If matter is therefore infinite and eternal, spirit is therefore infinite and eternal. The sooner scientists learn the fact that birth simply brings us into certain relations, and death takes us out of those relations, the better it will be for all who are concerned in this interesting subject.

The next item in that eloquent effusion is that man is "like the leaf," the mere "sport of destiny," returning in his "autumn" "to the elements of nature from which he sprang: dust to dust."

This orator asks the questions, "Whence came we?" "Whither are we tending?" "Who can tell?" To them he gives two answers. First, he says, "Some profess to know, but they know not." "The past is a mere sealed book." "The future is a blank." "Of the future, the hereafter, we are as ignorant as we are of the infinite conditions through which we have passed during the eternity which has preceded our brief present existences. If we could know the history of our past, we might get a glimpse of our future," "The past is a mere sealed book." Conclusion, "The future is a mere sealed book." The man is lost in the unbeliever's "narrow vale lying between two cold, bleak, barren eternities," viz: life. Lost (?) in the narrow vale. Yes! He knows nothing about his origin. He knows nothing about his destiny. So he says, and we have no right to contradict him. He is lost! But here he is again, listen! Speaking of the autumn leaves, he says, "LIKE US, they disappear and are merged into the ocean of matter from which they are evolved, ready to be RE-COMBINED into new forms of beauty." (Capitals mine.) Once more he says, "LIKE THAT LEAF which was the hope of spring, the pride and glory of summer, we are rudely torn away, the sport of destiny, to return to the elements of nature from which we sprung: dust to dust."

How he contradicts himself! But we must make all due allowances. He is in the presence of death. He says, "The past is beyond recall; the future is veiled in obscurity and in doubt; the present alone is ours." Here confusion is confounded; but let us ever remember that this was a funeral occasion, and the friends of the deceased were present, and this man Veveu was there, for the purpose, ostensibly, of giving a small amount of consolation to bereaved and broken hearts. Oh, how barren, how cold, how gloomy and God-dishonoring the consolation given! Those empty vessels of ours, hearts "endowed with inexhaustible hope," must turn away from the grave (?) *empty still*. No, not necessarily. God has provided a fountain. Go to it and fill your vessels. Let us not be too severe upon the man. There he stands amid bleeding hearts, and the open tomb just before him. Show pity, Lord! The man says, "No message ever reached man from beyond the grave." How very singular it is that many men repudiating God make a god of themselves. What kind of a being must I be to know that "no message ever reached man from beyond the grave?" How much must I know? Away back yonder in the past, in that "mere sealed book," is a grand and glorious message from beyond the grave. But to our friend it is a "sealed book."

What becomes of evolution?

What becomes of natural selection?

What becomes of the doctrine of the survival of the fittest?

THE MOTIVE THAT LED MEN TO ADOPT DARWINISM.

Before presenting the motive that led some of the great minds in unbelief to advocate the Darwinian theory of creation, it will not be amiss to remind the reader of the fact that the author of the "Vestiges of Creation" presented the evolution theory about twenty years before Mr. Darwin excited the public mind with the "hypothesis." Men who read the "Vestiges" looked upon the assumption as a speculation, but refused its adoption until Mr. Darwin, for the purpose of setting aside the idea of separate creations of species, improved so far upon the "Vestiges of Creation" as to repudiate design in nature. Having done this, many of the leading spirits in skepticism, with a few great minds in unbelief, at once accepted the wild speculation. Their motive may be seen in the following quotations: "The eye was not made for the purpose of seeing, or the ear for the purpose of hearing. Organisms, according to Darwin, are like grape-shot, of which one hits something and the rest fall wide." (Lay sermons, p. 331.) According to the above it appears that Huxley regarded the evolution of species, as advocated by Darwin, as identical with the old, effete idea that circumstances have determined everything. Buchner says, "According to Darwin the whole development is due to the gradual summation of innumerable minute and accidental operations." This is the same idea. Carl Vogt says, "Darwin's theory turns the Creator, and his occasional intervention in the revolutions of the earth and in the production of species, without any hesitation, out of doors, inasmuch as it does not leave the smallest room for the agency of such a being." Haeckel says, "The grand difficulty in the way of the mechanical theory was the occurrence of innumerable organisms, apparently, at least, indicative of design." He further says, "Some who could not believe in a creative and controlling mind, to get over the difficulty of apparent design, adopted the idea of a metaphysical ghost called vitality." He then presents his estimate of the service of Darwin in the following words: "The grand service rendered by Darwin to science is that his theory enables us to account for the appearances of design without assuming final causes, or, a mind working for a foreseen and intended end."

Strauss, after making the admission that the evolution theory is a mere guess, that it is no explanation of the cardinal points in descent, adds: "Nevertheless, as he has shown how miracles may be excluded, he is to be applauded as one of the greatest benefactors of the human race."—*Old Faith and New, p. 177.*

The same author says: "We philosophers and critical theologians have spoken well when we decreed the abolition of miracles; but our decree remained without effect, because we could not show them to be unnecessary, inasmuch as we were unable to indicate any natural force to take their place. Darwin has provided or indicated this natural force, this process of nature; he has opened the door through which a happier posterity may eject miracles forever."

Helmholtz says: "Adaptation in the formation of organisms may arise without the intervention of intelligence by the blind operation of natural law." This author confounds law with cause or agent. "Law is nothing without an agent to operate by it." Law is simply a rule of action. Let us hear Strauss once more: "Design in nature, especially in the department of living organisms, has ever been appealed to by those who desire to prove that the world is not SELF-EVOLVED (capitals mine), but the work of an intelligent Creator."—*Old Faith and New, p. 211.* On page 175 Strauss says of those who ridicule Darwin's evolution hypothesis and yet deny miracles: "How do they account for the origin of man, and, in general, the development of the organic out of the inorganic? Would they assume that the original man, as such, no matter how rough and unformed, but still a man, sprang immediately out of the inorganic, out of the sea or the slime of the Nile? They would hardly venture to say that; then they must know that there is only the choice between miracle, the divine hand of the Creator, and Darwin." According to this statement every man is left to one of three conclusions, viz:

1. That man came up immediately *as man* from the inorganic, or from the slime of the Nile, or from some other slimy place. Or,

2. That man was evolved from the lowest forms of life, according to Darwinism. Or,

3. That man was created by the divine hand, according to Christian belief.

Reader, which will you accept. Will you dethrone the Creator?

Choose you this day between the Creator and the slime of the sea with the sun's rays. What does Darwin know about the origin of life and mind? I am informed that he believes in a God, who, by miracle, gave the living unit at the base of his evolutionary series, but it seems to be an admission for the sake merely of avoiding disaster, for he says: "In what manner the mental powers were first developed in the lowest organisms is as *hopeless an inquiry* as how life itself *first originated.* These are problems for the distant future, if they are ever to be solved by man."—*Descent of Man, p. 66.* This is an open confession; in it all is given up.

I am now reminded of one of the last sayings of Strauss; here it is: "We demand for our universe the same piety which the devout man of old demanded for his God." This brings us to the same standard of piety. Then why the opposition?

Strauss denied a personal God. Of his mental condition we learn something from these words: "In the enormous machine of the universe, amid the incessant whirl and hiss of its jagged iron wheels, amid the deafening crash of its ponderous stamps and hammers—in the midst of this whole terrific commotion, man, a helpless and defenseless creature, finds himself placed, not secure for a moment, that on an imprudent motion a wheel may not seize and rend him, or a hammer crush him to a powder. This sense of abandonment is at first SOMETHING AWFUL." (Capitals mine.) Reader, the religion of Jesus Christ will save you from the terrible mental condition which is legitimate from a denial of God and his Christ. Will you accept it and experience the fact?

SHALL WE ABANDON OUR RELIGION?

There is no counterfeit without a genuine. Even a myth is related to something, near or remote, to which it bears some resemblance. There is nothing of great value that is not counterfeited. There is nothing that is not abused. Civil government has been wonderfully abused; in this respect it has fared no better than religion. There are many forms of civil government. There are many forms of religion. Let us ever seek the best form in each.

We are often pointed to the blood that has been shed in religious wars; but do unbelievers value civil government less because of the blood which they have cost? No. That blood speaks better things. May we not estimate civil government and religion both by the blood they have cost?

Unbelievers are very industrious in keeping before us the disagreements among Protestants. They say, Look! they can't agree among themselves. Well, is there any better agreement among politicians, or in civil governments? Is there any agreement among unbelievers which would serve as a model for us poor souls to imitate? I confess that the way is open for improvement among Protestants in this respect, but is it not just as open for a similar improvement among unbelievers in the scientific field of thought? There we find Atheists, Pantheists, Deists, Polytheists and Theists. In their history will be found an immense mass of contradictory opinions.

Man is imperfect in many of his attainments. A few men are more perfect than others, but all are liable to mistakes. Errors are found in all the histories of humanity; shall we therefore discard science and civil government? or shall we turn misanthropists? No; we will do neither. We are in a progressive age. We were capacitated for progression. We would not be men without this capacity. Let us ever remember that man is, after all his mistakes, the noblest creature of God, having God-like attributes. Do you doubt this? Then tell us why it is that a falsehood is always detestable to the mind. Why do men strenuously avoid contradictory propositions? The God-like in man is the great secret of his progression. He is a progressive being. Shall we on this account condemn all that in which man has and does progress? Shall we condemn Christianity on account of man's failures? Shall we discourage his honest efforts by keeping those failures always before him? Have men made no mistakes in science? Shall we repudiate on account of mistakes? Then there will be no end to repudiations. Let us remember and talk of the many mistakes that have been made in both science and religion, like the man "who visits the shadows in the deep ravines, in order that he may more fully realize the fact that the sun shines;" that is to say, let us talk of old, effete dogmas in science and in religion only to more fully realize the fact that the sunlight of truth is shining. Yes! Man has progressed. "Science and religion both stand true to their God." Man alone deviates. How often do we hear men say, "Science is progressive?" Scientific truth is always the same. Man is not always the same. Shall we keep his many deviations from truth and principle before him in order to cause greater deviations? Who will "deliver" the unbelievers of our country "from this dead body?" It contains all the errors of the ages. Their name is "legion." Among them we behold laws in the early history of our own country that to-day would shock the common sense of our country. Examine the old "Blue Laws of Connecticut." Among the errors of the past we find the "rack," the "thumb-screw," the "inquisition"—I was going to add the cross, but I recollect that unbelievers do not put that in their list. They do not sympathize with Christ, so they leave the cross out; in fact they do not like to talk about it. "It is their stumbling stone; the rock of their offense." I am tempted to say more about the errors of scientists in the bygone, but I must forbear; for in so doing I would ape the unbelievers. I have no great love for apes. So far as old, effete, erroneous opinions and faiths are concerned, with the old instruments of torture belonging to the shadows of the dark ages, we should say, disturb not the dead.

A man making his appearance among us as a lecturer, condemning all the sciences, presenting to the public mind the hundred and one old false ideas known in the history of scientific investigation, would be hissed out of literary circles.

An orator coming before the American people as a speaker, loaded with all the imperfections of our government, with its errors in legislation, its wicked and corrupt men accepting bribes, its mistakes on the fields of battle, resulting in great loss of life, as an open enemy to our country, breathing out treason, would subject himself to the anathemas of our government. The course pursued by unbelievers against the religion of Jesus Christ is without a parallel in the fields of science, civil governments and morals, yet the way is equally open in all those directions for a similar effort.

What is the value of the religion of Christ? What is the estimate placed upon it by the best minds of America? Andrew Jackson said, in his last hours, "That book, sir," pointing to the Bible, "is the rock on which our republic rests."

Benjamin Franklin said, "As to Jesus of Nazareth, my opinion of whom you particularly desire, I think the system of morals, and his religion, as he left them to us, is the best the world ever saw, or is likely to see."

John Adams said, "The Bible is the best book in the world."

Henry Clay said, "I always have had, and always shall have, a profound regard for Christianity, the religion of my fathers, and for its rites, its usages and observances."

U. S. Grant said, "Hold fast to the Bible as the sheet anchor of our liberties; write its precepts on your hearts, and practice them in your lives. To the influence of this book we are indebted for the progress made in true civilization, and to this we must look as our guide in the future."

General George Washington said, "It is impossible to govern the world without God. He must be worse than an infidel that lacks faith, and more than wicked that has not gratitude enough to acknowledge his obligation."

THE DOMAIN OR PROVINCE OF SCIENCE.

The Greeks used the word "epistasin" to express the idea that we express by the word science. Our word means certain knowledge. Theirs was understood to mean "coming to a stand," from "epi," upon, and "staseo," to stand. Science takes account of phenomenon and seeks its law. When you apprehend a phenomenon and discover its law you have accomplished all that the term indicates, even though you fail to comprehend the whys and wherefores of the law. "Certain knowledge," this phrase indicates limitation. All that it demands is that you know that which you profess to know. It therefore follows that the word "science" is equally applicable to the comprehensible and incomprehensible. The word is from "scio," *I know.* As men's knowledge, in the present state, at least, is limited, so science, as presented by man, is also limited; but, as men are progressive beings, science and the sciences may increase, adding more and more of truth. There are, however, shores beyond which science will never carry us, but on the contrary will leave us to settle down, to rest forever in content or discontent, just as we choose.

The modern hypothesis of materialistic unbelievers is that there is but one substance in the universe, and that is matter. If this be so, then all knowledge pertains to matter, and when you have reasoned yourself to the last element known, or knowable, in physical analysis, which will be the point of departure as well as your ultimate truth behind which you can not go, then, of course, you are where you must rest satisfied or dissatisfied; you have come to the Rubicon beyond which you will never pass. The mere physicist finds, as a legitimate result of his hypothesis of but one substance, his rest in the ultimate of eternal matter and blind force. The Christian, recognizing spiritual substance also, finds his ultimate or resting place in God, who is the last element in vital and mental analysis, and also the Christian's starting point in his inductive reasonings. We realize that scientific knowledge is profitable, even in the field of matter, but if we refuse to science any domain above matter she will lead us to the dust of the grave, there to forsake us forever amid its gloom and sorrow. Here Colonel Ingersoll's "night birds"—for angels he has no use—move with "rustling of wings." When such men reason themselves back to the germ cells and sperm cells, and stand there upon the last element in the analysis of the human body, they are not able to take another step until they acknowledge the existence of spiritual substance as matters master, which ever was, and is above matter, which takes hold of matter and builds germ cells and sperm cells and inhabits them, as the inherent fore which superintends the building, differentiating the species, and determining the sex.

Ask the unbeliever, the materialist, what this vital principle is, and he answers: "It is the all-pervading force that is modified by the organic structure." That is, in his philosophy, the "vital force is produced by the organism," and the "organism is produced by the vital principle?" So, being at the last limit of the physical analysis of the organic being, he is involved in a contradiction, while the Christian who believes in a spiritual substance refers all to spirit, and claims a continuation of his identity as an intelligent spirit, resting in his ultimate or starting point, viz: God. Do you say I am lost in God? Well, to be thus lost in God is to be saved from corruption and from the dust of the grave; but to be lost in the dust of the grave and in the ceaseless changes of matter is to be lost to God and to spiritual being. Let me be with God rather than lost amid the dark waves of oblivion.

Has science no prerogatives above the physical? Tread lightly here; you might step on holy ground. Do you use the old cry that all outside of matter belongs to the "unknown" and "unknowable?" Exchange the terms for the terms the "uncomprehended" and the "incomprehensible," and we will walk side by side. We know many things which we do not comprehend. Do we comprehend all that belongs to the physical sciences? Do we comprehend matter? I know that I know, but do I comprehend that knowledge? If I should say I know the unknowable, I am guilty of a contradiction in language. Do you say matter is infinite? Can I comprehended the infinite? If science be that certain knowledge which is the equivalent of comprehension, then one of two things is true: First, there is no such thing as physical science; or, secondly, I may have certain knowledge of the infinite—may comprehend the infinite. How is this? Where is the difficulty? It is here: the knowledge which constitutes science is not necessarily that knowledge which is the equivalent of the comprehension of the thing known. Hence the incomprehensible is not to be excluded from the field of scientific investigation. If matter be infinite, and if it belongs to the field of scientific knowledge, then the infinite and incomprehensible belong, also, to the domain of scientific investigation. If the infinite can not be comprehended, matter can not be comprehended, and if all that can not be comprehended should be dismissed from scientific investigation, then matter should be dismissed.

In physical science we know the vital force exists which builds the germ and sperm cells, but we do not comprehend it. If you ask physical science to explain this invisible force or power, she will say, Gentlemen, I have given you an introduction to this wonderful builder; you see it is there at the threshold of organic being, but I can not tell you why it is there, nor what its properties are; if it has any, they are outside of my domain. I deal with matter.

You must ask at the gate of the unseen, ask the science of the spiritual, the mental and vital. I am in wonderful contrast with mind, with life also. I am inertia. Some of my votaries have tried to give you the answer which you so much desire. They have said, "It is the all-pervading force which was lying away back in the antechambers of eternity." Have said, "It was burdened with a universe of worlds." Have said, "It was destitute of personality." Have said, "It was not, and is not, an intelligence." Have said, "It was without will, purpose or desire." Have said, "All beauty, harmony and order were its results." Have also said, "It was," away back in the ages past, groaning and heaving, travailing, in great anxiety to be delivered. Speaking of it in the light of "natural selection," they have deified it, giving to it all the mental operations of an intelligent, living God. On this account some of my lovers are Pantheists. They deify nature; deify everything, and call it all God. A few ignorant Christians, on this very account, are ready to give up their warfare with Pantheists. But the battle is not won because the word "God" is pronounced; for sober reason says, If nature is *all* God, she is *a* God, who is no God; or a nature without a God, just as you choose to express it. After all, it remains an axiom, that "you can not get more out of a thing than there is in it." So, of necessity, there must be, somewhere in this universe, *Eternal life and mind*. Reader, "how readest thou?"

BLIND FORCE OR INTELLIGENCE, WHICH?

In the discussion of this question I think it proper to submit a few axiomatic or common-sense truths which are universally admitted by the unbiased mind.

First. "Every effect must have a cause."

Secondly. "Every series must have a unit lying at its base."

Thirdly. "In every beginning there must be that which began."

Fourthly. "Something is eternal."

Fifthly. "There can not be an endless succession of dependent things."

Sixthly. "There must be that upon which the first dependent link in the chain of dependent things depended."

Seventhly. "That thing, whatever it may be, upon which the first dependent thing depended, must be eternal."

Was it blind force or intelligence, which?

The existence of a supreme intelligence is the first great leading thought made known in the Bible.

The first that is made known in unbelief, is the existence of "the unknown."

When a man adopts the idea of the unknown, he lays down all his strength to oppose the idea of a supreme intelligence, for what right has he to dogmatize about the unknown? The use of the word force will not help us to a better understanding of things. Force is simply the manifestation of energy, and there must, necessarily, be something lying behind it to which it, as an attribute or quality, belongs. That "something" the Bible calls "spirit." It has never been christened with a name by the unbeliever. Force is the bridge between it and matter, and the bridge between it and all things upon which it operates. The unbeliever's "unknown" lies behind force. Has he ever given it a name?

So far as science is concerned, it is paying her proper respect to say she demands an intelligence in order to account for the wonderful things with which she has to deal. Laycock, treating upon the questions of mind and brain, says: "The phenomena of life present a vast series of adjustments and modifications to fill certain purposes and bring about ends."—*Mind and Brain, vol. 1, p. 222 to 224.*

Systematic action in the use of means to accomplish certain ends or purposes we regard as the evidence of intelligence. By what other means do we distinguish between the rational and the insane? Winchel says, in his "Religion and Science," p. 102, "Without God we can not account for the correlation presented by the world of structural part to structural part, of structural part to intelligible end, of structural part to persistent plans or archetypes, of correlations which show that they were anticipated."

Beal, on Protoplasm, p. 104 to 107, says, "Living matter overcomes gravitation and resists and suspends chemical affinity." He adds, "It is in direct opposition to chemical affinities that organized beings exist."

What power is that which lies behind chemical affinities, and controls them with direct reference to organic being? Will some bold unbeliever answer?

Carpenter says, "The most universal and fundamental attribute of life is the mode of vital activity manifesting itself in the development of the germ into the complete organism and type OF ITS PARENT, and the after maintenance of the organism in its integrity at the expense of materials derived from external sources. The life in the germ is the controlling agency, superintending the building, charged with the working out the design of the architect." Who is the architect? Or, if you prefer it, what is the architect? Whoever he or whatever it may be, the design and decrees of nature are with that official. All the changes that can be made in environments or food will not change the organism from the type of its parent. Then the structure of the male and the female with reference to future living organisms, or procreation, is in very poor harmony with the idea that the architect is "blind force."

The same milk from one and the same animal, with the same heat and air, will build up bodies of different types, one as well as another, making human flesh in the human body, and dog's flesh in the dog's body, and sheep's flesh in the sheep's body. If the living germinal organism has its paternity in a dog, it will remain a dog in spite of food and environments.

Carpenter says, "The vital force," in the germ, "is not the entire force or means of growth; heat is a constructive stimulus, but amounts to nothing where there is no life. Food is material for the building, but like heat, it is of no consequence in the absence of life."

The constructing force in the germ manifests itself, in the plant, in the conversion of the insoluble starch of the seed into sugar, and in an additional change of a part of that sugar so as to set at liberty a large amount of carbon, which, uniting with the oxygen of the air, forms carbonic acid, and this process is attended with a liberation of heat which supplies the germ with stimulus.

"It is different with the advanced plant. The organic compounds required to extend the fabric, are formed by the plant, instead of being supplied from without. The tissues of the green surface of the stem and leaves have the peculiar power, when acted on by light, of generating, at the expense of carbonic acid, water and ammonia, with various ternary and quarternary organic compounds, such as chlorophyll, starch, oil and albumen. A part goes to build new tissues, and a part is stored up in the cavities of tissues for food for parts to be developed in the future." Mr. Carpenter says, "Of the source of this peculiar power we have no right to speak confidently." Is it a blind force that anticipates growth in the plant, and lays away food, in the tissues, for future use? Why should it be different with the young plant?

Sixteen simple substances are known to exist in vegetable organisms, and many of them are more strongly inclined to unite with substances which have no existence in vegetable cells; so they separate, in violation of chemical laws, and unite in vegetable cells in utter disregard of the affinities which are known to be their strongest. How do unbelievers manage such objections to the hypothesis that chemical laws explain everything in vegetable life? How is all this accounted for? We, Christians, answer, "The course of nature is the art of God." This answer is equivalent to the thought that vegetable life is the result of the union existing between God and the vegetable kingdom. The force that lies behind all chemical affinities and controls them, together with the wisdom displayed in that kingdom, belongs to God.

SPECIES, OR UNITS OF NATURE.

Are millions of years adequate as a cause, when associated with all the forces known in nature, to produce new species and extirpate old ones? The teachings of Darwin require an answer in the affirmative.

The survival of the fittest is one of Darwin's emphasized laws of natural selection. He says: "In all cases the new and improved forms of life tend to supplant the old and unimproved forms. New varieties continually take the place of and supplant the parent form. New and improved varieties will inevitably supplant and exterminate the older."—*Origin of Species, pp. 264, 266, 413.*

Do the facts sustain this assumption? The little animals whose remains compose the great chalk-beds are alive and working. Inarticulate or molluscan life is seen in a sub-fossil condition in the Post Pliocene clays of Canada. They are just as they were in the beginning of their history. Species seem to be immutably fixed. The demand for millions of years, in order to get old species out and new ones in, breaks down with the mollusk of the Pliocene in the clays of Canada. The Pliocene species are the more recent; such is, in fact, the meaning of the term in geology. The mollusk of Canada Pliocene clay has undergone no change since its first appearance upon our globe.

In order to account for ancient life, that passed away, as far back as the carboniferous age, it is claimed that millions of years passed before that age began. But here are the very first species of mollusca in the more recent clays unchanged, and here are the same little animals that floored so much territory in the bygone with chalk. How does this look by the side of the last quotation from Darwin?

Crabs or lobsters, cuttle-fish, jelly-fish, star-fish, oysters, snails, and worms lived contemporary with the first vertebrates. I have recently read an article in which it is said by an advocate of the Darwinian hypothesis, that man in his original condition was a cannibal, feasting, ordinarily, upon snails and worms. Now, it is claimed that millions of years have passed, and that millions of years inevitably destroy old species and introduce new ones; and yet here are the same old pesky snails and worms. If millions of years have passed the system is false. And if millions of years have not passed the system is false; so it is certainly false.

Hybrids are wonderfully in the way of the hypothesis. They can not be saved. All artificial varieties return to their simple form. Mr. Huxley recognizes this as an objection that can not be surmounted. He says, "While it remains Darwin's doctrine, must be content to remain a mere hypothesis;" that is, a mere guess.

In the latest productions of Agassiz we have this statement: "As a palæontologist I have from the beginning stood aloof from this new theory of transmutation, now so widely admitted; its doctrines, in fact, contradict what the animal forms buried in the rocky strata of our earth tell us of their own introduction and succession upon the surface of the globe."

The first vertebrates are sharks, ganoids and garpikes, which are the highest in structure of all known fishes. Darwin's hypothesis demands this order *reversed*.

When you ask an evolutionist for the links connecting new and old species, as he is pleased to denominate them, you receive the satisfactory (?) answer, "They are lost." A painter presented a man with a red canvass, claiming that it represented the children of Israel crossing the Red sea. The question was asked, "Where are the Israelites?" The painter answered, "They have crossed over." "But," said the man, "where are the Egyptians?" "O, my dear sir," said the artist, "they are under the sea." This is a very fine illustration of facts, if Darwinism may boast of facts, for the connecting links between species are "under the sea" of oblivion, never to be found, and the old species "have passed over." Mr. Darwin's apology is in these words: "Every one will admit that the geological record is imperfect; but very few can believe that it is so very imperfect as my theory demands." This is a grand concession. The "wild speculation" has no support from geology. The blanket of oblivion, which Mr. Darwin and his friends spread over the difficulty, is "millions of years." In that length of time the missing species, or links, would, of course, all pass out of sight. Is this true? No. In the geological record millions of specimens are fossilized and laid away in nature's great cabinet. Why not find a few of the missing links there? Just one. "One fact, gentlemen, if you please." Science is certain knowledge. Is there certain knowledge of missing links? Gentlemen, just bridge one gulf for us; the gulf lying between any *two species* will do. We get impatient, standing and gazing. Look! Can you see across?

Mr. Darwin says, "Professor Haeckel, in his general Morphology and other works, has brought his great knowledge and abilities to bear on what he calls phylogeny or the lines of descent of all organic beings."—*Origin of Species, p. 381.*

This author, Mr. Haeckel, has "lines of descent" which involves the idea of a plurality of beginnings in the history of organic being; that is, Mr. Haeckel claims a vertebrate series with a vertebrate lying at the base of the series, and an articulate series with an articulate lying at its base. So there must be A SPECIAL CREATION AT LAST. Hear him: "There appears, indeed, to be a limit given to the adaptability of every organism by the type of its tribe or phylum. Thus, for example, no vertebrate animal can acquire the ventral nerve chord of articulate animals instead of the characteristic spinal marrow of the vertebrate animals."—*History of Creation, vol. 1, p. 250.* So the vertebrate must forever remain a vertebrate, and the articulate forever an articulate. Were they both evolved from the same unit? We are anxious to know, how from a pulpy mass of flesh, from a moneron, a creature of one substance, *vertebrates* were evolved. We would like to know, also, how a creature of more than one substance could be evolved from a creature of one substance without more being gotten out of the thing than there was in it. Here spontaneous generation passes into a wreck. Do you see? The pulpy mass of flesh, or moneron, from which so much has been "evolved" was the result of "the sun's rays falling upon the sea slime," and was and is a creature of one substance, homogeneous. "Natural selection" could not operate in the vertebrate type before it existed. It was "limited to the type or phylum." That is to say, natural selection could evolve new species without limitation from each type, but could never evolve a vertebrate from an articulate, nor an articulate from a vertebrate. Then, how are the two series from the same unit; or, if they are connected with two different units, how are those units the effect of the same unintelligent cause? How are we going to cross this chasm lying between the sun's rays and the sea slime upon the one hand, and the articulate and the vertebrate upon the other? Darwin says, "Judging from the past, we may safely infer that not one living species will transmit its unaltered likeness to a distant futurity." Well, how is it with the past? We are told that millions of years are the demand for the changes already brought about. Millions of years would certainly be enough to constitute a "distant futurity." How is it now? Is there not one species having its likeness represented by a species in the distant past? Yes; the genus lingula, the species appearing in all the ages, was "connected by an unbroken series of generations from the lowest Silurian stratum to the present day."—*Origin of Species, pp. 293, 294, 428.*

Darwin's "theory" claims that the first forms of all life still exist, and are known and named. The ape, if it could talk like a man, would boast of a history reaching all the way back to time prior to the existence of the greater number of the mammals. To get rid of the difficulty of first forms still existing, Mr. Darwin cuts off his unit from the law of "the survival of the fittest," or "the inevitable destruction of the parent form." He says: "A very simple form, fitted for very simple conditions of life, might remain for indefinite ages unaltered, or unimproved; for what would it profit an infusorial animalcule, or an intestinal worm, to become highly organized?"— *Animals and Plants, vol. 1, p. 19.* "Under very simple conditions of life a higher organism would be of no service."—*Origin of Species, p. 100.*

How are we to reconcile the conflicting ideas in this speculation? At one time we are taught that all forms of life were, originally, very simple forms, existing under very simple conditions. At another time we are taught that "new and improved forms *inevitably* supplant and destroy parent forms." At another we are taught, at great length, the doctrine of the survival of the fittest.

At another we are taught that all things have worked, and do work, without designs upon the part of a present intelligence.

At another we are taught that very simple forms of life, under the very simple conditions of life, have continued to the present day, because of the fact that it would be of NO SERVICE for them to become highly organized. No service to whom? To what end?

Out of thine own mouth will I condemn thee. What! Is there an end in view that has governed in the great question of evolution of species, and the survival of the fittest? Darwin seems to think so. The wonderful "machine" that Strauss talked about in connection with the "smashing" and "crashing" that destroys parent forms did not smash the simplest forms of life. Why? The answer is, "It would be of no service for them to become highly organized." Then all the smashing and crashing known in the doctrine of "the survival of the fittest" and in "the destruction of the parent form" was under the supervision of some controlling power, having an end to accomplish.

If we see a member of the church of Christ living in obedience to the "law of Christ," we say he is a Christian, and speak of him as such; on the other hand, if we know he is in works denying Christ, being disobedient, we tacitly assume that he is not a Christian, yet a *mawkish charity* keeps us, in too many instances, from speaking out in this matter, and also keeps us from earnestly trying to distinguish the true Christian; and this is one of the great sins of the church in our times, for thus the wicked are not put to shame, and others are caused to hesitate in their graces by the conduct of those whom, in mawk charity, are called Christians.

"Mouth-glue is made of pure glue, as parchment glue, or gelatine and coarse brown sugar. Take pure glue and add one-quarter or one-third of its weight of brown sugar. Put both into a sufficient quantity of water to boil and reduce the mass to a liquid, then cast into thin cakes on a flat surface *very slightly* oiled, and, as it cools, cut up into pieces of a convenient size. When you wish to use it moisten one end in the mouth, and rub it on any substance

you wish to join; a piece kept in the work-box is very convenient."—
Chambers.

The Christian's faith was not intended to sit him down in ease, but to stimulate him to the discharge of his duties. So the work of faith is a noble work, a life of labor.

MISCELLANEOUS.

The oft-repeated story that man had his beginning in a low state of barbarous cannibalism is a groundless assumption.

What is the difference between getting more out of a thing than there is in it and creating something out of nothing?

"If the religious foundations and sanctions of morality are to be given up, what is to be substituted for them?"—*Lord Selborne.*

The Orang and Pongo monkeys, which are classed with those which make the nearest approach to man, have three vertebra fewer than man.

"Live while we may;" "Let us eat and drink, for tomorrow we die," are natural corollaries from the teachings of modern as well as ancient infidels.

Finding human skeletons with the skeletons of extinct animals necessitates the bringing of those animals forward, for specimens have been found in modern times with the flesh upon their bones and food in their stomachs.

If all organized animal life was evolved from the moneron, a creature of one substance, homogeneous, how were creatures of more than one substance evolved without more being *evolved* than was *involved*? Let some of our scientific "wise-acres" solve this problem.

Paul says, "Things which are seen were not made of things which do appear." Every negative has its affirmative. The affirmative of the above is this, "Things which are seen were made of unseen things." The Bible does not teach that anything was made of nothing.

The Chimpanzee has thirteen pair of movable thoracic ribs. Man has two. If man lived up in the bushes, like the Chimpanzee and other apes, he would need more movable ribs so that he might not be ruined by broken ribs every time he might happen to fall. Is there no evidence of design here?

All unbelievers who advocate the idea of spontaneous generation try to get more out of matter than there was in it, viz: life, sensation, intelligence and moral nature. Can you get more out of a thing than there is in it? Is there life without antecedent life, etc.? Unbeliever, are you mocking the Bible because somebody said the Lord created something of nothing, and at the same time advocating spontaneous generation, and thereby professing to get more *evolved* than was *involved*?

The idea that stone implements are an index to man in the beginning of his existence is an unwarranted conceit; they may point to a degeneracy. The lost arts are indicative of that which might have been repeated many times. Stone implements might have been used, as we know they have been, in times of great civilization. They are an uncertain index of civilization among the tribes who used them, and no index of the civilization of other tribes who lived at the same time in other parts of the earth.

Professor Huxley says, "I understand and I respect the meaning of the word soul, as used by Pagan and Christian philosophers, for what they believe to be the imperishable seat of human personality, bearing throughout eternity its burden of woe, or its capacity for adoration and love. I confess that my dull moral sense does not enable me to see anything base or selfish in the desire for future life among the spirits of the just made perfect; or even among a few poor fallible souls as one has known here below."—*Modern Symposium, vol. 1, p. 82.*

CPSIA information can be obtained
at www.ICGtesting.com
Printed in the USA
BVHW071951011121
620451BV00002B/338

9 789355 344885